ANIMALS AND THEIR WORLD

SALLY MORGAN

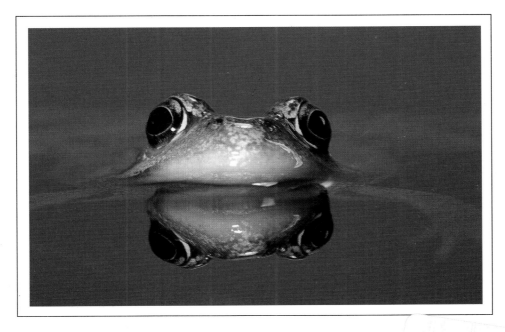

KING**f**ISHER

BOSTON

KINGFISHER
a Houghton Mifflin Company imprint
222 Berkeley Street
Boston, Massachusetts 02116
www.houghtonmifflinbooks.com

First published in 1996
This edition first published in 2001
10 9 8 7 6 5 4 3 2

2TR/0607/WKT/(RNB)/128MA/F

LIBRARY OF CONGRESS CATALOGING-IN-
PUBLICATION DATA
Morgan, Sally.
Animals and their world / Sally Morgan.—
1st ed.
    p.   cm.—(Young discoverers)
Includes index.
Summary: Presents information about how
animals use their senses to communicate, find
food, protect themselves, and more. Includes
related activities.
   1. Senses and sensation—Juvenile literature.
[1. Animals—Physiology. 2. Senses and
sensation.] I. Title II. Series.
QP434.M67   1996
591.1'82—dc20 96-12455 CIP AC

ISBN 978-0-7534-5498-5

Editor: Molly Perham
Designer: John Jamieson
Art editor: Val Wright
Consultant: Michael Chinery
Photo research: Elaine Willis
Illustrations: Peter Bull p. 9 (top left & right),
11 (top), 15 (top), 17 (right), 19 (bot. right),
23 (top right), 29 (bot.); Joanne Cowne p. 21
(right), 27 (bot.), 28 (bot.); Angelica Elsebach
p. 7 (bot. right), 12 (bot. left), 13 (top left),
16 (top left), 27 (top); Nick Hall p. 8-9, 23
(bot. right); Ian Jackson p. 8 (top right), 10
(left), 10-11, 16-17, 18 (left), 18-19, 19 (top
right), 20 (left), 23 (top left), 26 (left), 28 (top
right), 30 (left), 31 (top left and right); Stuart
Lafford p. 30-31; Adam Marshall p. 4-5, 12-
13, 14 (left), 14-15, 16 (bot. right), 17 (bot.
left), 20-1; Eric Robson p. 22-23; Phil Weare
p. 26 (center), 29 (top); Ann Winterbotham p.
6 (left), 6-7, 7 (top right), 24-25.
Photographs: Bruce Coleman p. 13 (Jane
Burton), 26 (Fred Bruemmer); NHPA p. 6 (Ivan
Polunin), 10,12 (Stephen Dalton), 18 (G J
Cambridge), 22 (E A Jones), 25 (Dave
Watts), 28 (Michael Leach), 30 (Manfred
Danegger); Nature Photographers Ltd p. 14
(Michael Gore), 20 (Paul Sterry).

Printed in China

About This Book

This book looks at how different kinds of animals are adapted to survive in different environments. It explains how animals communicate, and how they use their senses to search for food and to avoid predators. It also suggests lots of experiments and things to look for. You can carry out all the experiments either in your home, in your yard, or in a park or nearby woodland.

Activity Hints

- Before you begin an experiment, read through the instructions carefully and collect all the things you need.
- When you have finished, put everything away and wash your hands.
- Start a special notebook so that you can keep a record of what you do in each experiment and the things you find out.

Contents

The Animal Kingdom

Animals range in size from tiny creatures that can only be seen under a microscope to the huge blue whale. They may look very different from one another, but animals have many features in common. Sight, hearing, smell, taste, and touch allow them to communicate and to be aware of their surroundings. These senses also help animals to find food, which gives them the energy to move and to find a mate, so that they can reproduce.

How Many Types?

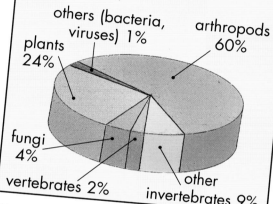

There are 1.5 million types of living organisms. Animals are the largest group, and they are divided into vertebrates (with backbones) and invertebrates (without backbones). Arthropods are the largest group of invertebrates.

others (bacteria, viruses) 1%

arthropods 60%

plants 24%

fungi 4%

vertebrates 2%

other invertebrates 9%

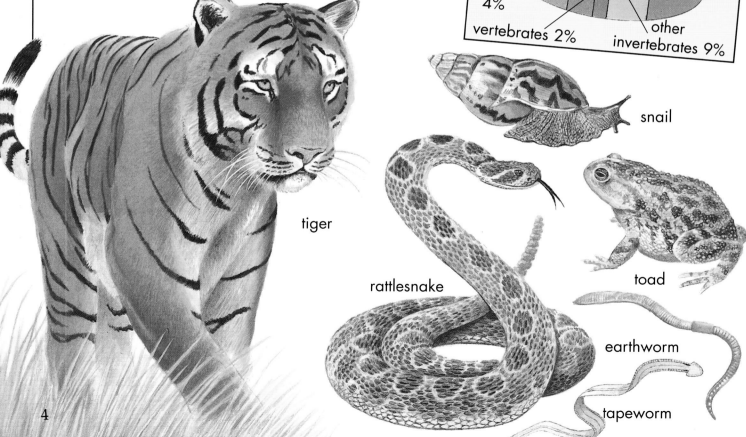

tiger

snail

rattlesnake

toad

earthworm

tapeworm

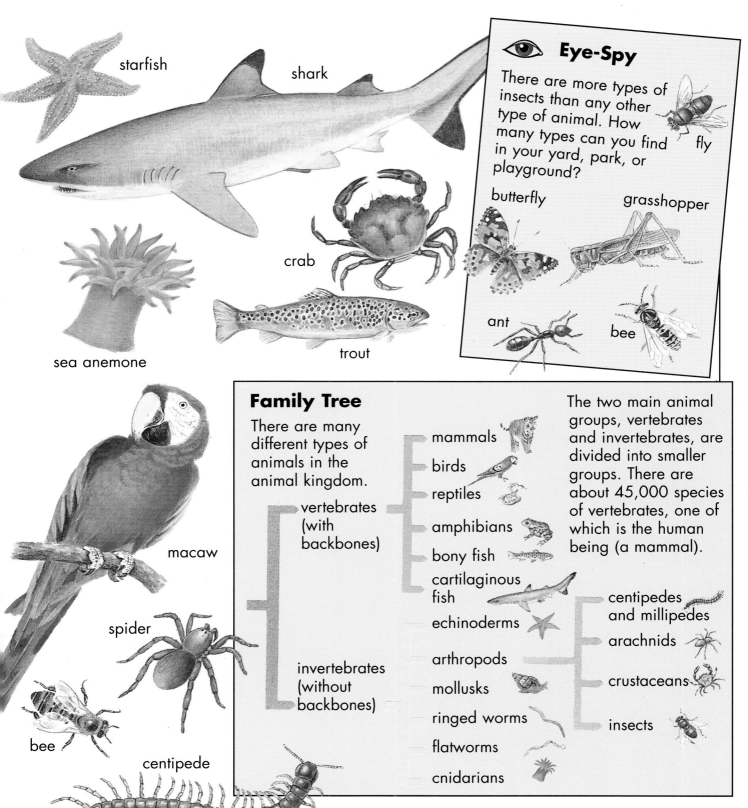

starfish

shark

sea anemone

crab

trout

macaw

spider

bee

centipede

👁 Eye-Spy

There are more types of insects than any other type of animal. How many types can you find in your yard, park, or playground?

fly

butterfly

grasshopper

ant

bee

Family Tree

There are many different types of animals in the animal kingdom.

The two main animal groups, vertebrates and invertebrates, are divided into smaller groups. There are about 45,000 species of vertebrates, one of which is the human being (a mammal).

vertebrates (with backbones)
- mammals
- birds
- reptiles
- amphibians
- bony fish
- cartilaginous fish

invertebrates (without backbones)
- echinoderms
- arthropods
  - centipedes and millipedes
  - arachnids
  - crustaceans
  - insects
- mollusks
- ringed worms
- flatworms
- cnidarians

5

Communication

Animals communicate by sight, smell, touch, hearing, and even electrical signals. They send signals to tell other animals that they have found a new source of food, and they send special alarm signals if they sense danger. One of the most important roles of communication is to bring male and female animals together. Many male birds have brightly colored feathers or sing beautiful songs to attract the females.

Making Light

On a summer night, a female glowworm climbs a tall grass stem and signals to a male glow-worm with her brightly lit abdomen.

Color Talks

A cuttlefish communicates by using color. It changes the color of its skin to send messages to other cuttlefish. A red color indicates anger. This is used by one male to warn off another.

butterfly

jaguar

In the shadowy darkness of the jungle, animals have to advertise their presence with bright colors, or by sounds.

poison-arrow frog

6

uakari monkey

howler monkey

macaw

toucan

tree frog

Dance of the Honeybee

A honeybee tells other bees where to find food by dancing. It performs a "waggle dance" in a figure eight. This special dance tells the other bees how much food there is and in which direction to fly.

Do it yourself

Biologists learn a lot about animal communication by observing their behavior.

Watch your pet and record your observations. See how it communicates by its behavior. When your cat is in a friendly or playful mood, it will hold its tail erect.

The Brain and Nervous System

Animals need fast links between their senses and their muscles so that they can move, search for food, and avoid predators. The nervous system connects the senses to the brain, which receives information from all over the body. The brain analyzes the information and sends a message back to tell the muscles to move. The largest part of a vertebrate's brain is the forebrain, or cerebrum. Mammals have a much larger cerebrum than any other kind of animal. Different parts of the cerebrum control the senses, memory, and intelligence.

Blinking

Blinking is an automatic reflex. Mammals do it without thinking. Each time a mammal blinks, the eyes are washed with a fluid, keeping them free from germs.

Eye-Spy

When you catch a ball, your body reacts quickly because of reflexes. These are automatic responses that you do not have to think about. Try to notice the different reflexes you use each day.

Large and small brains

Stegosaurus was 29 feet (9 m) long and weighed about 1.75 tons. Yet this dinosaur's brain was only the size of a walnut, weighing just 2.5 ounces (70 g). A human brain weighs about 3 pounds (1.4 kg).

brain

Chimpanzees have learned to use a stick as a tool to dig termites from their nest. This method of feeding involves the senses of sight, touch, and taste. Their brain coordinates the actions.

Do it yourself

Build a maze and see how long it takes your pet mouse or hamster to find some food.

1. To make the walls, cut some corrugated cardboard into strips about 6 inches (15 cm) wide. Hold them in place on a large board with tape or glue.

corrugated cardboard

2. Place a little food at the center of the maze. Put your pet at the entrance to the maze. It will use the senses of sight and smell to find the food.

food

9

Sight

Sight is the sense that helps animals to observe their environment, find food, and see other animals. Most animals have two eyes, each giving a slightly different image. Predatory mammals have eyes at the front of their head so that both eyes can focus on one object. The brain compares the views from each eye to produce a three-dimensional image that allows the mammal to judge the distance and speed of its prey. Many animals have eyes on the sides of their head, to give good all-around vision that alerts them to attackers.

Compound Eyes

Insects have compound eyes made up of thousands of tiny, separate lenses. The large compound eyes of this dragonfly help it to be an efficient hunter.

vulture

lion

jackal

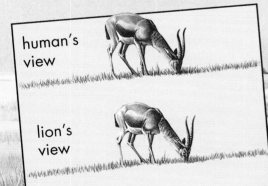

human's view

lion's view

Seeing in Color

A human looking at a gazelle sees a full color image. A lion looking at a gazelle sees only shades of black and white.

10

Do it yourself

Your eyes can play tricks on you. Try this trick to "behead" a friend!

1. Ask your friend to stand against a wall. Close your right eye. With your left eye focus on a point about 3 feet (1 m) to the right of her head.

2. Walk toward your friend and keep looking at the point.

3. All of a sudden, you will notice out of the corner of your eye that your friend's face has disappeared.

How It Works

When you are a certain distance away from your friend, the light from her face falls on the "blind spot" in your eye. This spot is where the optic nerve leaves the eye, so there are no cells to detect the light. Because the brain receives no information about light falling here, it cannot see the face.

harp eyesight is important n the wide open plains of e African savanna. Lions find nd chase their prey, while vultures hover bove on the lookout for their next meal.

zebras

hyena

The chameleon's eyes move independently. One can look forward while the other looks backward. This allows the chameleon to be aware of predators approaching from almost any direction.

 Eye Spy

When you step outside at night, you cannot see much at first. Gradually, your eyes start to get used to the dark, and you begin to see more objects. It takes your eyes about 20 minutes to get properly adjusted.

Owls have excellent sight. These nocturnal birds fly at night when there is only the light from the moon. They have large, round eyes to collect as much light as possible. Their sight is so good that they can spot a mouse moving through the grass from high up in the sky. Owls also have very flexible necks and can turn their head through three-fourths of a circle.

Eye-Spy

Nocturnal animals, such as owls and foxes, have a special layer at the back of their eyes that reflects light. You can see these animals at night in the headlights of a car. When the light catches their eyes, you will see the "eye-shine" in the beam as pairs of blue or orange dots.

When frogs float at the surface of a pond, their large eyes protrude above the water. Their eyes have good all-around vision and are particularly sensitive to the movement of flying insects. This is useful for catching food or sensing any danger.

Hearing

Sound is made by something vibrating. The movement creates sound waves that travel through air, water, and solid objects. A mammal's ear is more developed than the ear of a fish or bird. It has three parts—the outer, middle, and inner ear. The outer ear funnels sound waves into the head. The middle ear has three tiny bones that magnify the sound. The inner ear is filled with a fluid. Sound waves cause the fluid to push on nerve endings, sending a message to the brain.

African guinea fowl can hear the sound of thunder hundreds of miles away. This tells them that rain is on the way.

At night in the desert, sound carries well. Animals that come out in the cool of the night have excellent hearing, which enables them to find food and to hear predators.

coyote

Strange Ears

Not all animals have ears on their heads. Crickets have ears on their knees, and cockroaches' ears are on their tails. Spiders have no ears at all. Special hairs on their legs and feet can detect sound vibrations.

cricket

cockroach

spider

jack rabbit

14

Do it yourself

Having two ears allows us to judge the direction of sounds. See what happens when you use only one ear.

1. Place a blindfold over your eyes and cover one ear.

2. Ask a friend to stand a short distance away and tap a hollow object with a stick. Can you tell from which direction the sound came?

More Things to Try

How good is your hearing? Ask your friend to drop a small object to the ground. Then get them to drop it farther away. How far away can you still hear the sound of the object hitting the ground?

kit fox

Large Ears

To improve their hearing, people cup their hands behind their ears. This makes a funnel to catch more sound waves. Rabbits have large ears for the same reason.

Many animals have a hearing range that is greater than our own—they can hear sounds that we cannot. Dog trainers use a whistle that to us makes no sound, but it can be heard by a dog. Sometimes we can hear these sounds by using special sound recorders. We cannot hear the ultra-sonic noises made by bats, but they can be picked up by an electronic bat detector that alters the sound so that we can hear it.

Hearing Under Water

Dolphins produce sound waves that travel through water. The sound waves bounce off fish and this tells the dolphins where to hunt. Fishing boats use sonar in the same way.

Elephants make loud trumpeting noises, and they also communicate with their stomachs! Their stomachs produce very low growling sounds that humans cannot hear. These sounds travel great distances over the grasslands and can be heard by elephants far away.

Do it yourself

An animal's sense of balance comes from its ears.

Squirrels have to be able to keep their balance when climbing and jumping, or they would fall to the ground.

You can lose your balance if you spin around too quickly. You can prevent this by "spotting." Pick an object on the wall and focus on this as you spin. Does this stop you feeling dizzy?

Seeing With Sound

Bats have excellent hearing and use it to navigate and hunt in the dark. A bat emits very high frequency sounds that bounce off walls and other objects, forming an echo. The bat's ears pick up the echoes. The bat can then work out the position of objects, including flying moths.

echo

high frequency sounds

How It Works

Spinning around confuses your sense of balance. By focusing on a fixed spot, your brain receives extra information from your eyes.

17

Smell

When we smell something, we are detecting traces of substances in the air. As we breathe in, the air passes over special sensors in the nose. Humans can distinguish between 10,000 different smells, and dogs can detect even more. Predatory animals rely on their sense of smell to find food. Polar bears can detect the rotting body of a seal on the ice more than 12 miles (20km) away. Some animals have a sense of smell, but do not have noses. Lizards and snakes use their darting tongue to collect smell samples from the air.

Pheromones

Moths communicate by releasing chemicals called pheromones. Their antennae are so good at detecting pheromones in the air that one moth can follow the scent trail of another over great distances.

Sniffer Dogs

The long shape of a dog's nose encourages air to circulate around the most sensitive parts, giving the dog a good sense of smell. Some dogs are trained to sniff out drugs concealed in baggage.

The giant anteater has an excellent sense of smell, which it uses to find its favorite food, termites.

Marking Territory

Deer mark trees and shrubs around the edge of their territory with a scent that lingers for many days. This warns other deer to keep out.

Do it yourself

A scent becomes less noticeable as you get used to it.

1. Dab perfume on your arm. You can detect it easily. Can you smell it after an hour?

2. Can your friend smell the scent after an hour? Your smell receptors have become used to the smell and lost their sensitivity to it, but to your friend the scent is new.

19

Taste

The sense of taste comes from taste buds on the tongue, inside the cheek, on the roof of the mouth, and in the throat. Humans can only distinguish between four basic tastes—sweet, sour, salty, and bitter—but when these are combined with a sense of smell, we can distinguish between many different foods. Animals that live in water often have a particularly well-developed sense of taste. Deep-sea fish have poor sight, and some of them rely on taste-sensitive filaments that hang from their mouths.

Butterflies have special taste sensors on their feet. Female butterflies use them to make sure that they lay their eggs on the right kind of leaf.

Taste Buds

Not all mammals have the same number of taste buds. Pigs have about 15,000 taste buds —almost twice as many as humans.

shark

spiny lobster

Sea anemones and octopuses have taste cells on their tentacles, and sharks have them in their mouth. The spiny lobster has a pair of antennae that can smell and taste rotting flesh.

octopus

Do it yourself

Find out which food the birds in your yard prefer.

1. Put two different foods, such as breadcrumbs and sunflower seeds, into two containers. Place them on a bird-table or on an outside ledge. Hang a bag of peanuts from the table.

2. In a notebook, record which species of birds visit and what food they eat. Do they come at a regular time? Do they have a favorite food? You may need a bird watcher's book and a pair of binoculars to help you identify all the different birds.

sunflower seeds

breadcrumbs

peanuts

More Things to Try

Try some more hanging food, such as pine cones with peanut butter smeared between the scales, pine cones filled with suet, or a chain of peanuts in their shells. Other foods that you could put in the containers are mealworms, small pieces of cheese, or chopped-up apples.

sea anemone

Touch

The sense of touch is triggered by pressure on an animal's skin or outer covering. This stimulates receptors that send messages along the nerves to the brain. A mammal's skin has millions of receptors for light and heavy pressure, hot and cold, and pain. Some areas, such as the fingertips, are more sensitive than others. Fish are very sensitive to changes in water pressure. A line of touch receptors, called the lateral line, runs along their bodies.

Birds have whiskerlike feathers on their wing tips that provide information about air currents. This helps them to control their flight.

Cave dwellers have a well-developed sense of touch to find their way in the dark. Spiders and other arthropods have extra long legs or special antennae. The salamander has nerves that are sensitive to vibrations. Cave fish have additional receptors on their head and tail so they can "feel" their way around.

cricket

spider

millipede

centipede

blind shrimp

salamander

Whiskers

Moles have sensitive whiskers around their mouths. They can even sense a draft of air caused by a wriggling worm. Whiskers on the tail tell a mole about the size and shape of a tunnel.

Do it yourself

Discover which part of the skin is the most sensitive.

Blindfold a friend. Hold two pencils with the tips close together. Touch the tips on the skin of the forearm, the back of the arm, the palm, and the back of the hand. Can your friend feel one or two pencil tips?

How It Works

An area of skin with touch receptors close together is very sensitive. Two pencils touch two receptors, so the brain detects two tips. If the receptors are fewer and farther apart, the skin is less sensitive and one of the tips may not be close enough to a receptor to trigger it.

Fingertips

Gorillas have sensitive fingertips with many touch receptors. These help gorillas to groom each other. Grooming removes fleas and strengthens the bond between parent and offspring.

blind cave fish

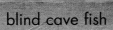

23

A Sixth Sense

Many animals have senses that we have only just begun to understand. Using these senses, they may view the world very differently from the way we see it. The Earth has an invisible magnetic field that causes a compass to point to north. Some animals can detect this and use the information to navigate. Many fish have special organs that can generate an electrical charge. They use these organs to find their way around and even to stun their prey.

Animals often seem to behave strangely just before a disaster, such as an earthquake, strikes. Cats carry their kittens to safety, and snakes and rats flee from buildings. These animals can sense changes in the environment that humans are not yet aware of.

Seeing the Heat

The rattlesnake has poor eyesight, but at night it can detect mice moving from several yards away. It has a sense organ on its head that can "see" the body heat of its prey.

24

The Platypus

The platypus lives in murky rivers of Australia. It hunts at night, using a special sense organ in its bill to detect the electrical activity produced by the muscles of its prey.

Homing Pigeons

Pigeons are good navigators. They can still find their way home—even if they are released hundreds of miles away. It is not clear how they navigate, but scientists think that they may be sensitive to the Earth's magnetic field.

In the fall, many birds prepare to migrate. As the time to depart gets closer, they become very active. Watch for them in the early evening, flying over in huge flocks.

Some animals travel great distances to find food or to migrate to warmer climates. They may navigate by using magnetic fields, or even the position of the moon and stars. Salmon swim across thousands of miles of ocean and find their way to the river in which they were born, where they will then lay their eggs. Scientists think they can taste the water and detect the chemicals unique to their home river.

A female turtle migrates across the ocean to lay her eggs on a particular beach. After a few weeks, the baby turtles hatch and make the dangerous journey across the sand to the ocean.

Migrating Butterflies

Every fall, millions of monarch butterflies fly south from Canada to California and Texas. They spend the winter roosting on trees and bushes. In spring, they fly north again to lay eggs.

A Sense of Time

At the equator, the length of day and night changes very little throughout the year. Farther north and south, there are distinct changes that produce the seasons. Animals living in these areas are affected by both the changing length of day and the temperature. Many animals breed in spring, because there is plenty of food and their young have time to grow before the onset of winter. Some animals avoid bad weather by migrating to a warmer place, or by hibernating. A hibernating animal goes into a deep sleep in winter; its body temperature falls and its heart rate slows down to conserve energy.

Eye-Spy

Birds use all sorts of materials to make their nests. Often they gather garbage such as pieces of net and string. Sometimes they build their nests in mailboxes, on telephone poles, or in old metal drums. Look for birds using unusual materials and nesting in odd places.

Spring is a busy time for animals. Birds build their nests and lay their eggs. Mammals such as cows and sheep give birth to their young.

27

As well as the seasons, the regular pattern of day and night affects many animals. Diurnal animals are active during the day and sleep at night. Nocturnal animals do the opposite. Animals that live on the seashore are strongly influenced by the tides. Some only come out to feed when they are covered by water. At low tide they stay hidden under rocks.

The North American brown bear survives the long cold winters by sleeping in a cave or under a fallen tree.

Eye-Spy

Dawn can be a very noisy time. More birds sing at first light than at any other time of the day.

Hunting at Night

The fox is a nocturnal animal. It has well-developed senses for finding food in the dark.

28

Rhythms of the Tides

The fiddler crab has a "body clock" to measure the timing of the tides. At low tide it emerges from its burrow to hunt for food.

The crab instinctively knows when the tide will change and when it has to return to the burrow.

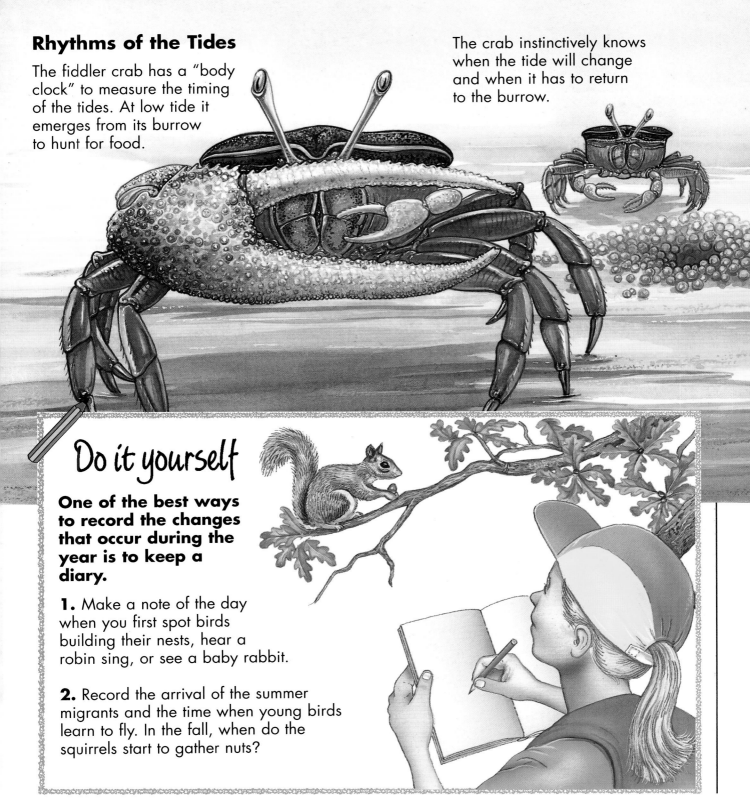

Do it yourself

One of the best ways to record the changes that occur during the year is to keep a diary.

1. Make a note of the day when you first spot birds building their nests, hear a robin sing, or see a baby rabbit.

2. Record the arrival of the summer migrants and the time when young birds learn to fly. In the fall, when do the squirrels start to gather nuts?

Learning and Instinct

Animals are born with natural instincts that help them to survive. Newborn foals can get up and run within minutes. Birds instinctively know how to build their first nest and care for their young. But other patterns of behavior are learned by watching adults or by trying things out. For example, an animal will learn which food is good to eat and where to find it, and which foods make it feel ill.

Young cheetahs learn to hunt by watching their mother and hunting with her. They practice hunting techniques during play with their brothers and sisters.

👁 Eye-Spy

Look out for young animals learning to do something for the first time. It could be young birds taking their first flight, or a kitten playing with a new toy.

First Impressions

A gosling fixes attention on the first thing it sees moving when it hatches from the egg. This instinctive behavior is called imprinting.

Do it yourself

A biologist called Pavlov trained dogs to link the sound of a bell with food.

You can try this with any pet, even goldfish.

Every time you feed your pet, ring a small bell first.

1.

2. Within a few days, your pet will link the sound of the bell with food, and will come up to you as soon as it hears the sound.

Chicks instinctively open their beaks to receive food from their mother, but they will have to learn where to find food and how to fly. A spider has a natural instinct to spin a web. Amazing isn't it?

Index